2024 MacBook Pro M4 User Guide

Exploring the M4 Chip's Potential

Daryl Ackerman

Table of Contents

Introduction

Overview of the 2024 MacBook Pro

On October 30, 2024, Apple unveiled its latest iteration of the MacBook Pro, a device that continues to set the standard for high-performance laptops. The 2024 MacBook Pro is equipped with the groundbreaking M4 chip, which promises to enhance both speed and efficiency across a variety of professional applications. With preorders already underway and a full release scheduled for November 8, this new model is generating considerable excitement among developers, engineers, and creative professionals alike.

The 2024 MacBook Pro comes in three configurations: the base model featuring the M4 chip, and two higher-end versions powered by the M4 Pro and M4 Max chips. This strategic differentiation allows Apple to cater to a wide range of users—from casual professionals who require robust performance for everyday tasks to those engaged in intensive graphics work or complex data modeling.

Apple's commitment to innovation is evident not only in the processing power of the new MacBook Pro but also in its design and features. The laptops boast a sleek aesthetic available in black or silver, and they come equipped with advanced connectivity options including Thunderbolt 5 ports, HDMI output for up to 8K resolution, and an SDXC card slot. Additionally, the inclusion of a MagSafe 3 charging port enhances usability for on-the-go professionals.

The display technology has also received significant upgrades. The new models feature a nano-texture screen designed to deliver clearer images even in bright conditions, making them ideal for outdoor use. With a peak brightness of up to 1,600 nits in HDR mode, these displays are perfect for tasks requiring high color accuracy and detail.

With all these advancements, the 2024 MacBook Pro is positioned as not just a laptop but as an essential tool for professionals aiming to maximize their productivity and creativity.

Significance of the M4 Chip

At the heart of the 2024 MacBook Pro is Apple's latest silicon innovation—the M4 chip. Built using cutting-edge 3-nanometer technology, this chip represents a significant leap forward in performance and efficiency compared to its predecessor, the M3. The M4 chip features an impressive architecture that includes a 10-core CPU with up to four high-performance cores and six efficiency cores. This configuration allows it to handle demanding tasks with ease while optimizing power consumption.

One of the most notable advancements of the M4 chip is its GPU capabilities. It incorporates a 10-core GPU that leverages Apple's next-generation graphics architecture. This GPU not only enhances graphical performance but also introduces features such as Dynamic Caching and hardware-accelerated ray tracing—capabilities that were previously reserved for high-end desktop systems. These enhancements make the M4 chip particularly suitable for graphics-intensive applications like video editing, gaming, and 3D rendering.

Moreover, the M4 chip boasts Apple's most powerful Neural Engine yet, capable of performing up to 38 trillion operations per second. This level of processing power enables sophisticated machine learning tasks and artificial intelligence applications directly on the device, eliminating latency issues often associated with cloud computing. As AI continues to play an increasingly critical role across various industries, having such capabilities integrated into a laptop will empower users to harness AI tools more effectively in their workflows.

The significance of the M4 chip extends beyond raw performance metrics; it embodies Apple's vision of creating an ecosystem where hardware and software work seamlessly together. The integration of advanced machine learning capabilities allows applications to leverage AI functionalities such as real-time image processing, natural language understanding, and predictive analytics—all executed locally on the device.

In summary, the introduction of the M4 chip not only enhances the performance profile of the MacBook Pro but also reinforces Apple's commitment to pushing technological boundaries. As professionals increasingly rely on their laptops for complex tasks that demand both speed and efficiency, the M4-equipped MacBook Pro stands out as a formidable contender in the market.

Performance Enhancements

The performance enhancements brought by the M4 chip are particularly noteworthy when considering professional workflows that demand high levels of computational power. Benchmarks indicate that the M4 chip can deliver up to 1.5 times faster CPU performance compared to its predecessor while maintaining exceptional energy efficiency. This means that users can expect faster processing times for tasks ranging from software development to multimedia editing without sacrificing battery life.

In practical terms, this translates into significant time savings for professionals who rely on their devices for intensive tasks. For instance, video editors can render complex projects more quickly, while software developers can compile code faster than ever before. The enhanced multi-threaded capabilities also mean that users can run multiple demanding applications simultaneously without experiencing lag or slowdowns.

AI Capabilities

As artificial intelligence becomes more integrated into everyday applications, having a powerful neural engine is essential for maximizing productivity. The M4's neural engine is designed specifically to handle AI workloads efficiently. With its ability to perform trillions of operations per second, it enables features such as real-time translation in communication apps or advanced image recognition in photo editing software.

This capability not only enhances user experience but also opens doors for new applications that leverage AI technologies directly on-device—allowing creative professionals to innovate without being constrained by hardware limitations.

The introduction of the 2024 MacBook Pro marks another milestone in Apple's journey toward redefining personal computing through advanced silicon technology. With its powerful M4 chip at the core, this laptop is engineered not just for today's demands but also for future challenges in various professional fields.

As users prepare to embrace this new model, they can look forward to unparalleled performance improvements across all aspects—be it design aesthetics or computational capabilities—making it an indispensable tool for anyone serious about their craft. Whether you are a developer pushing boundaries in software creation or a designer crafting stunning visuals, the 2024 MacBook Pro promises to elevate your work experience significantly.

Chapter 1: Design and Aesthetics

New Color Options and Design Tweaks

The 2024 MacBook Pro not only brings significant advancements in performance with its M4 chip but also introduces a refined design that enhances both aesthetics and functionality. Apple has long been recognized for its commitment to sleek, minimalist design, and this latest iteration continues that tradition while also incorporating new elements that cater to the evolving needs of its professional user base.

One of the most notable changes in the design of the 2024 MacBook Pro is the introduction of a new color option: space black. This addition complements the existing silver finish, providing users with more choices to reflect their style. The space black variant offers a modern and sophisticated look that appeals to professionals who prefer a more understated yet elegant aesthetic. This color choice not only enhances the visual appeal of the device but also aligns with current trends in tech aesthetics, where darker hues are increasingly favored for their sleekness and versatility.

The overall design of the MacBook Pro remains true to Apple's iconic form factor, characterized by clean lines and a premium aluminum chassis. However, subtle tweaks have been made to improve usability. For example, the 14-inch model now features an additional USB-C/Thunderbolt 4 port on the right-hand side, addressing user feedback for more connectivity options without compromising the laptop's slim profile. This small yet impactful change allows users to connect multiple peripherals simultaneously, enhancing productivity for those who rely on various devices in their workflow.

The hinge mechanism has also been refined to provide a smoother opening experience while maintaining stability when typing or using the touchpad. This attention to detail ensures that the MacBook Pro not only looks good but feels good to use as well. The keyboard layout remains unchanged from previous models, featuring a comfortable typing experience with well-spaced keys and a responsive touchpad that enhances navigation.

In addition to functional tweaks, Apple has made strides in sustainability with this new model. The aluminum used in the chassis is sourced from recycled materials, demonstrating Apple's commitment to reducing its environmental footprint while maintaining high-quality standards. This focus on sustainability resonates with consumers who are increasingly conscious of their purchasing decisions and their impact on the planet.

Overall, the design and color options of the 2024 MacBook Pro reflect Apple's dedication to creating products that are not only powerful but also visually appealing and environmentally responsible. The combination of aesthetic elegance and practical enhancements positions this laptop as a top choice for professionals seeking both style and substance in their computing devices.

Display Enhancements: Nano-Texture and Brightness

One of the standout features of the 2024 MacBook Pro is its display technology, which has seen significant improvements designed to enhance user experience across various lighting conditions. Apple has incorporated a nano-texture screen option, which is particularly beneficial for professionals who often work in bright environments or outdoors.

The nano-texture glass technology minimizes glare without sacrificing brightness or color accuracy. This innovation is crucial for creative professionals such as photographers, videographers, and graphic designers who require precise color representation and detail in their work. The nano-texture surface scatters light in such a way that reflections are significantly reduced, allowing users to view their content even under direct sunlight or harsh indoor lighting conditions.

In addition to glare reduction, the display offers impressive brightness levels, peaking at an astonishing 1,600 nits in HDR mode. This level of brightness ensures that images appear vibrant and lifelike, making it ideal for tasks that demand high visual fidelity. Whether editing photos with intricate details or watching high-definition videos, users can expect an immersive experience that showcases every nuance.

The display also supports a wide color gamut (P3), which means it can reproduce a broader spectrum of colors compared to standard displays. This feature is particularly important for professionals working in fields such as video production or digital art where color accuracy is paramount. With support for True Tone technology, the display automatically adjusts its white balance based on ambient lighting conditions, ensuring that colors appear consistent regardless of where you are working.

Furthermore, Apple has integrated ProMotion technology into the display of the 2024 MacBook Pro. This feature allows for adaptive refresh rates up to 120Hz, resulting in smoother scrolling and more responsive interactions when navigating through applications or web pages. For creatives working with animation or video editing software, this responsiveness can significantly enhance workflow efficiency by providing real-time feedback during editing processes.

The combination of nano-texture glass, high brightness levels, wide color gamut support, and ProMotion technology makes the display of the 2024 MacBook Pro one of its most compelling features. It not only meets but exceeds the expectations of professionals who depend on their laptops for critical visual tasks.

User Experience: Functionality Meets Aesthetics

While aesthetics play a crucial role in attracting users to a device like the MacBook Pro, functionality is equally important. Apple has ensured that every aspect of the design contributes positively to the user experience. The thin bezels surrounding the display maximize screen real estate while maintaining portability—a key consideration for professionals who often work on the go.

The keyboard features backlit keys that adjust automatically based on ambient light conditions, ensuring optimal visibility regardless of lighting situations. The Touch Bar has been replaced with function keys in this iteration; however, users still benefit from customizable shortcuts through macOS's built-in features. This change reflects user feedback favoring tactile feedback over touch-sensitive controls during intensive workflows.

Apple's commitment to sound quality is also evident in this model. The speakers have been enhanced to deliver richer audio with improved bass response—ideal for media consumption or video conferencing. Coupled with advanced microphone arrays that reduce background noise during calls or recordings, users can expect clear communication whether they are collaborating remotely or presenting ideas in meetings.

The design and aesthetics of the 2024 MacBook Pro represent a harmonious blend of style and functionality tailored specifically for professionals. With new color options like space black adding sophistication alongside practical enhancements such as additional ports and refined usability features, Apple continues to set benchmarks in laptop design.

The display improvements—featuring nano-texture glass technology and exceptional brightness—underscore Apple's commitment to providing tools that enhance creativity and productivity while ensuring comfort during extended use.

As users embrace this latest iteration of the MacBook Pro, they will find themselves equipped with an elegant yet powerful device capable of meeting their diverse needs—whether they are designing graphics, editing videos, or engaging in software development—all while enjoying an aesthetically pleasing experience that reflects their professional identity.

Chapter 2: Performance Improvements

M4 Chip Architecture and Specifications

The 2024 MacBook Pro is powered by Apple's latest M4 chip, a significant advancement in the company's silicon technology that promises to redefine performance standards in portable computing. Built on a second-generation 3-nanometer process, the M4 chip integrates cutting-edge architecture designed to maximize both efficiency and power. This architecture employs a "big. LITTLE" configuration, featuring a combination of high-performance cores and energy-efficient cores that work together seamlessly to handle a wide range of tasks.

Core Configuration

The M4 chip boasts a robust 10-core CPU, comprising four high-performance cores and six efficiency cores. This configuration allows the chip to deliver exceptional performance for demanding applications while conserving

18

energy during less intensive tasks. The high-performance cores are optimized for speed, making them ideal for resource-heavy applications such as video editing, software development, and gaming. In contrast, the efficiency cores handle lighter workloads, ensuring that users can enjoy extended battery life without sacrificing performance.

The architecture of the M4 chip includes enhancements such as improved branch prediction and wider decode and execution engines for the performance cores. These improvements result in faster processing times and better overall responsiveness. The efficiency cores also benefit from a deeper execution engine, allowing them to manage background tasks effectively while keeping power consumption low.

Neural Engine and GPU

In addition to its CPU capabilities, the M4 chip features a powerful 10-core GPU that elevates graphics performance to new heights. This GPU is designed for demanding visual tasks such as 3D rendering, gaming, and video playback. It supports advanced technologies like hardware-accelerated ray tracing and mesh shading, which enhance the realism of graphics by simulating how light interacts with objects in a scene.

Furthermore, the M4 includes a 16-core Neural Engine capable of performing up to 38 trillion operations per second. This makes it exceptionally well-suited for machine learning tasks and artificial intelligence applications. The integration of this Neural Engine allows developers to create more sophisticated applications that leverage AI capabilities directly on the device, reducing reliance on cloud processing and improving responsiveness.

Transistor Density and Efficiency

With 28 billion transistors packed into its compact design, the M4 chip represents a significant leap in transistor density compared to previous generations. This increase not only enhances performance but also contributes to energy efficiency—an essential factor for mobile devices where battery life is paramount. The advanced manufacturing process enables Apple to optimize power consumption while delivering high-speed performance, ensuring that users can rely on their devices for extended periods without needing frequent recharges.

Performance Metrics: CPU and GPU Advancements

The real-world performance of the M4 chip is where its advancements become particularly evident. Benchmarks indicate that the M4 chip outperforms its predecessor, the M3, by approximately 10% to 20% in both single-threaded and multi-threaded tasks. This improvement positions the M4 chip as a formidable competitor against high-end x86 processors from Intel and AMD.

CPU Performance

In terms of CPU performance, users can expect faster processing times across various applications. Tasks such as compiling code or rendering graphics benefit significantly from the enhanced clock speeds of the M4's performance cores, which can reach up to 4.4 GHz. This boost in clock speed translates into quicker execution of complex calculations and improved multitasking capabilities.

For professionals engaged in data-intensive workflows—such as video editing or software development—the ability to run multiple demanding applications simultaneously without lag is crucial. The M4's architecture allows it to handle these scenarios with ease, providing users with a smooth experience even under heavy workloads.

GPU Performance

The GPU advancements in the M4 chip are equally impressive. With its 10-core design, the GPU delivers stunning graphics performance that rivals dedicated graphics cards in many respects. For instance, it can handle external displays with resolutions up to 6K, making it an excellent choice for creative professionals who require high-resolution output for their work.

Moreover, the GPU's support for hardware-accelerated ray tracing enhances visual fidelity in gaming and professional applications alike. This technology simulates realistic lighting effects by calculating how light interacts with surfaces in real time, resulting in more immersive experiences for users.

In gaming scenarios, benchmarks show that the M4's GPU can outperform entry-level dedicated GPUs like NVIDIA's GeForce RTX 3050 Ti in short bursts of activity. However, it's important to note that sustained performance during long gaming sessions may be affected by thermal throttling due to the lack of active cooling in ultra-thin devices like the MacBook Pro.

Thermal Management

Apple has prioritized thermal management within its design philosophy for the M4 chip. The efficient architecture allows for lower power consumption during typical use cases, which helps mitigate heat generation. While there are inherent limitations when it comes to sustained high-performance tasks—such as gaming or extensive video rendering—the intelligent design ensures that users can engage in demanding activities without experiencing significant overheating issues.

Real-World Applications

The advancements brought by the M4 chip translate into tangible benefits across various professional domains:

- **Creative Professionals:** For photographers and videographers using software like Adobe Premiere Pro or Final Cut Pro, the enhanced CPU and GPU capabilities mean faster rendering times and smoother playback during editing sessions.

- **Software Developers:** Developers working with integrated development environments (IDEs) will find that compiling large codebases is significantly quicker with the M4's superior processing power.

- **Gamers:** Casual gamers will appreciate the improved graphics quality and frame rates offered by the M4's GPU when playing modern titles or engaging in graphics-intensive applications.

The introduction of Apple's M4 chip marks a pivotal moment in mobile computing technology. With its innovative architecture combining high-performance and efficiency cores, alongside an advanced GPU and Neural Engine, this chip sets new benchmarks for what users can expect from their devices.

As professionals across various fields embrace this new technology within the 2024 MacBook Pro, they will find themselves equipped with tools capable of handling even the most demanding tasks with ease. Whether it's creating stunning visuals, developing complex software solutions, or engaging in immersive gaming experiences, the M4 chip empowers users to push boundaries like never before.

In summary, Apple's commitment to innovation is evident not only in raw performance metrics but also in how these advancements enhance everyday workflows for professionals around the globe. As we look forward to future developments within Apple's silicon lineup, one thing is clear: the M4 chip has set a new standard for excellence in mobile computing.

Chapter 3: AI Features and Capabilities

Introduction to Apple Intelligence

In the ever-evolving landscape of technology, artificial intelligence (AI) has emerged as a transformative force, reshaping how we interact with our devices. Apple, a leader in innovation, has taken a significant step forward with the introduction of **Apple Intelligence**, an integrated AI system designed to enhance user experience across its ecosystem of devices, including iPhones, iPads, and Macs. Officially unveiled during the 2024 Apple Event, Apple Intelligence aims to redefine personal computing by providing users with intelligent assistance that is both proactive and contextually aware.

Apple Intelligence is built on the foundation of advanced machine learning algorithms and generative models, allowing it to understand and anticipate user needs in real-time. Unlike traditional AI systems that rely heavily on voice commands or specific inputs, Apple

Intelligence operates in the background, analyzing user behavior and preferences to offer personalized suggestions and automate routine tasks. This seamless integration into the Apple ecosystem enhances usability, efficiency, and overall device performance.

One of the standout features of Apple Intelligence is its focus on **privacy**. In a world where data security is paramount, Apple has designed this AI system to prioritize user privacy by processing most data on-device rather than relying on cloud-based solutions. This approach not only ensures that sensitive information remains secure but also allows for faster response times and a more intuitive user experience.

As Apple continues to innovate, Apple Intelligence represents a new era of personal AI that enhances everyday tasks while maintaining the company's commitment to privacy and security. With features designed to streamline workflows and improve productivity, Apple Intelligence is poised to become an indispensable tool for users across various domains.

Neural Engine Enhancements for AI Workloads

At the heart of Apple Intelligence lies the **Neural Engine**, a specialized component within Apple's silicon architecture that significantly enhances the device's ability to perform AI-related tasks. The Neural Engine is designed to handle complex computations required for machine learning and artificial intelligence applications efficiently. With each generation of Apple silicon, including the M4 chip featured in the 2024 MacBook Pro, enhancements have been made that allow for faster processing of AI workloads.

The latest Neural Engine boasts an impressive capability of performing up to **38 trillion operations per second**, making it one of the most powerful components available in consumer electronics today. This level of performance enables real-time processing of data for various applications, from natural language understanding to image recognition and beyond.

Key Enhancements in Neural Engine Functionality

1. **Natural Language Processing (NLP)**: The advancements in the Neural Engine have significantly improved its ability to understand and generate human language. This enhancement allows Apple Intelligence to provide context-aware responses, making interactions with Siri more natural and fluid. Users can now engage in multi-turn conversations where Siri remembers previous questions and maintains context throughout the dialogue.

2. **Image Recognition**: The enhanced Neural Engine also excels at image processing tasks. With its ability to analyze visual data rapidly, Apple Intelligence can recognize objects, people, and scenes within photos and videos. This capability not only improves photo organization but also enables features like automatic tagging and intelligent search functions—users can search their photo library using natural language queries such as "photos from last summer" or "pictures with my dog."

3. **Smart Task Automation**: One of the most impactful applications of the Neural

Engine is its role in automating everyday tasks. By learning user habits and preferences over time, Apple Intelligence can suggest actions or perform tasks without requiring explicit commands. For example, if a user typically sets reminders for workouts at 7 AM every day, Apple Intelligence may proactively suggest this reminder when it detects that the user is awake.

4. **Generative Capabilities**: The Neural Engine's generative capabilities allow it to create content based on user input. Whether it's drafting emails, generating summaries of long articles, or even creating custom images based on text prompts, these features empower users to express themselves creatively while saving time on mundane tasks.

5. **Enhanced Siri Integration**: With deeper integration into Apple Intelligence, Siri has undergone a significant transformation. The combination of improved language understanding and contextual awareness allows Siri to provide more relevant suggestions based on user behavior. For instance, if a user frequently asks about weather updates before leaving for work, Siri

can proactively provide this information without being prompted.

6. **Real-Time Transcription**: In applications like Notes or during phone calls, users can record audio that is automatically transcribed into text summaries post-call or meeting. This feature not only aids in capturing important information but also enhances productivity by allowing users to focus on discussions rather than note-taking.

Privacy Considerations

Apple's commitment to privacy is woven into the fabric of its AI capabilities. By leveraging on-device processing through the Neural Engine, sensitive data remains secure without being transmitted over the Internet for analysis. This approach minimizes risks associated with data breaches while ensuring that users retain control over their personal information.

Additionally, features like **Private Cloud Compute** allow for more complex computations without compromising privacy. When necessary tasks require additional resources beyond what can be handled on-device, anonymized data can be processed securely in Apple's cloud infrastructure without exposing individual user information.

Real-World Applications of Apple Intelligence

The capabilities provided by Apple Intelligence are not just theoretical; they translate into practical applications that enhance daily life for users:

- **Productivity Tools**: For professionals who rely on email communication and scheduling tools, Apple Intelligence streamlines workflows by prioritizing important messages in their inboxes and suggesting timely responses based on previous interactions.

- **Creative Expression**: Artists and content creators can utilize generative tools within Apple Intelligence to brainstorm ideas or create visual content quickly. For example, users can describe a scene they want illustrated or request design variations based on specific parameters.

- **Enhanced Communication**: With improved transcription capabilities during calls or meetings, teams can maintain focus on discussions while receiving accurate summaries afterward—ensuring that critical points are captured without distraction.

- **Personalization Across Devices**: As users engage with multiple devices within the Apple ecosystem—iPhone, iPad, Mac—the continuity provided by Apple Intelligence ensures that preferences are synchronized seamlessly across platforms. This integration creates a cohesive experience where users feel understood regardless of which device they are using.

Apple Intelligence represents a significant leap forward in how artificial intelligence can enhance everyday interactions with technology. By integrating powerful machine learning capabilities directly into its devices through advanced Neural Engine enhancements, Apple has created an ecosystem where AI works intelligently behind the scenes—anticipating needs and streamlining workflows without compromising privacy.

As users begin to explore the full range of features offered by Apple Intelligence—from smart task automation to generative content creation—they will find themselves equipped with tools that not only simplify their digital lives but also empower them creatively and professionally.

In this new era of personal AI, Apple continues to set standards for innovation while prioritizing user privacy—a commitment that resonates deeply in today's digital landscape where data security is paramount. As we look ahead at future developments within this framework, it's clear that Apple Intelligence will play an integral role in shaping how we interact with technology moving forward—making our devices smarter while enhancing our daily lives in meaningful ways.

Chapter 4: Model Variants and Configurations

Overview of the Three MacBook Pro Models

The 2024 MacBook Pro lineup introduces three distinct models, each powered by Apple's latest M4 family of chips: the base M4, the M4 Pro, and the M4 Max. These models cater to a diverse range of professional needs, from everyday tasks to demanding workflows in creative and technical fields.

1. **14-Inch MacBook Pro with M4**:
   - The entry-level model, starting at $1,599, is equipped with the M4 chip, featuring a **10-core CPU** that includes **six efficiency cores** and **four performance cores**. This configuration is designed to handle typical productivity tasks such as web browsing, document editing, and light media consumption with ease.
   - The M4 also includes a **10-core GPU**, providing sufficient graphical power for casual gaming and basic video editing. With support for up to **32GB of unified memory**, this

model is ideal for users who require a capable machine for everyday use without the need for high-end performance.

2. **14-Inch and 16-Inch MacBook Pro with M4 Pro**:
   - Starting at $1,999 for the 14-inch version and $2,499 for the 16-inch version, the M4 Pro model is aimed at professionals who engage in more demanding tasks. It features a **14-core CPU** comprising **10 performance cores** and **four efficiency cores**, which significantly boosts processing power for tasks such as software development, video editing, and graphic design.
   - The GPU configuration is enhanced to include a **20-core GPU**, allowing for improved graphics performance suitable for creative professionals working with high-resolution images or complex animations. Users can configure this model with up to **64GB of unified memory**, making it a powerful option for multitasking and running resource-intensive applications.

3. **14-Inch and 16-Inch MacBook Pro with M4 Max**:
   - The flagship model starts at $2,499 for the 14-inch variant and $2,999 for the 16-inch

variant. It is designed for users who require the utmost performance in their workflows. The M4 Max features a robust **16-core CPU**, which includes **12 performance cores** and **four efficiency cores**, delivering exceptional processing capabilities that can handle extensive computational tasks effortlessly.

- With an impressive **40-core GPU**, the M4 Max excels in graphics-intensive applications such as 3D rendering, gaming, and video production. This model supports up to **128GB of unified memory**, providing ample resources for professionals working with large datasets or complex software environments.

Key Differences Between M4, M4 Pro, and M4 Max

While all three models share a common foundation in Apple's innovative silicon architecture, they differ significantly in terms of performance capabilities, memory options, and intended use cases.

CPU Performance

- **M4 Chip**: The base model's 10-core CPU delivers solid performance suitable for general productivity tasks. It provides up to 1.5 times faster CPU performance compared to its predecessor (the M2), making it an excellent choice for everyday users who engage in light multitasking.

- **M4 Pro Chip**: With its enhanced 14-core CPU configuration, the M4 Pro offers substantial improvements in processing speed—up to 2.1 times faster than leading competitors in similar categories. This makes it ideal for professionals who work with demanding applications like video editing software or programming environments.

- **M4 Max Chip**: The most powerful option features a 16-core CPU that can achieve speeds up to 2.5 times faster than comparable PC chips. This chip is tailored for users engaged in high-performance computing tasks such as scientific simulations or extensive data analysis.

GPU Performance

- **M4 Chip**: The integrated 10-core GPU provides adequate graphical capabilities for casual gaming and basic multimedia tasks. It supports hardware-accelerated ray tracing but is best suited for less demanding applications.

- **M4 Pro Chip**: The upgraded 20-core GPU significantly enhances graphics performance, making this model suitable for creative professionals working on projects that require higher fidelity graphics or real-time rendering capabilities.

- **M4 Max Chip**: With its powerhouse 40-core GPU, the M4 Max offers unparalleled graphics performance that can handle heavy-duty tasks like 3D modeling and video production with ease. It is particularly beneficial for professionals in fields such as animation or game development where visual fidelity is crucial.

Memory Options

- **M4 Chip**: This model supports up to 32GB of unified memory, which is sufficient for most everyday tasks but may become limiting when running multiple resource-intensive applications simultaneously.

- **M4 Pro Chip**: Users can configure this model with up to 64GB of unified memory—an essential feature for professionals who require additional memory capacity when multitasking or working with large files.

- **M4 Max Chip**: The flagship model stands out with support for up to an astounding 128GB of unified memory. This capability allows users to run multiple high-demand applications concurrently without experiencing slowdowns—ideal for video editors working with high-resolution footage or data scientists analyzing large datasets.

Media Engine Enhancements

All three models benefit from Apple's advanced Media Engine technology; however, there are notable differences:

- The basic M4 includes essential media encoding capabilities but lacks specialized hardware acceleration features found in the higher-end models.

- The M4 Pro features enhanced media encoding engines that support multiple codecs including H.264 and HEVC, making it more adept at handling video production workflows.

- The M4 Max takes this further by incorporating dedicated hardware accelerators specifically designed for professional media workflows. It includes two video encode engines and two ProRes accelerators that significantly expedite video processing tasks—essential for filmmakers and content creators who demand high efficiency in their editing processes.

Target User Profiles

Understanding the key differences between these models helps potential buyers identify which MacBook Pro best suits their needs:

1. **Casual Users**: Those who primarily use their laptops for web browsing, streaming media, and basic productivity tasks will find the base M4 model adequate. Its performance capabilities are more than sufficient for everyday activities without breaking the bank.

2. **Creative Professionals**: Graphic designers, video editors, and software developers will benefit from the enhanced capabilities of the M4 Pro model. Its balance of power and efficiency makes it ideal for those who require reliable performance without needing top-tier specifications.

3. **Power Users**: For professionals engaged in high-performance computing tasks—such as data analysis, scientific research, or advanced content creation—the M4 Max is unmatched. Its superior processing power and memory capacity cater to those whose workflows demand peak performance at all times.

The introduction of the three distinct MacBook Pro models—powered by Apple's cutting-edge M4 family of chips—marks a significant evolution in portable computing technology. Each variant caters to different user needs while maintaining Apple's commitment to quality and innovation.

From casual users seeking an efficient laptop for everyday tasks to creative professionals requiring robust performance capabilities and power users needing maximum processing power, there is a MacBook Pro model tailored specifically to meet those demands.

As technology continues to advance rapidly, Apple's strategic approach in offering differentiated models ensures that every user can find a device that aligns perfectly with their workflow requirements—making the 2024 MacBook Pro lineup not just a series of laptops but rather versatile tools designed to empower creativity and productivity across various fields.

Chapter 5: Connectivity Options

Thunderbolt 4 and 5 Ports

The 2024 MacBook Pro lineup represents a significant leap in connectivity options, particularly with the introduction of **Thunderbolt 4** and **Thunderbolt 5** ports. These advanced interfaces are designed to enhance the user experience by providing faster data transfer rates, improved compatibility with a wide range of devices, and the ability to connect multiple peripherals simultaneously.

Thunderbolt 4: A Versatile Connectivity Standard

Thunderbolt 4 is a robust connectivity standard that builds upon the capabilities of its predecessor, Thunderbolt 3. It offers several key features that enhance usability for professionals and everyday users alike:

1. **High-Speed Data Transfer**: Thunderbolt 4 supports data transfer speeds of up to **40

Gbps**, enabling rapid file transfers between devices. This high bandwidth is particularly beneficial for users who frequently work with large files, such as video editors or graphic designers.

2. **Daisy-Chaining Capabilities**: One of the standout features of Thunderbolt technology is its ability to daisy-chain multiple devices together. Users can connect up to **six Thunderbolt devices** in a single chain, simplifying cable management and reducing clutter on desks.

3. **Display Support**: Thunderbolt 4 ports can support up to two **4K displays** at 60Hz or a single **8K display**, making them ideal for professionals who require high-resolution screens for their work. This capability is essential for tasks that demand high visual fidelity, such as video editing or graphic design.

4. **Power Delivery**: Thunderbolt 4 supports power delivery up to **100W**, allowing users to charge their devices quickly while simultaneously transferring data. This feature is particularly advantageous for those who rely on their laptops for extended periods without access to power outlets.

5. **Universal Compatibility**: Thunderbolt 4 is fully compatible with USB-C, meaning users can connect to a wide range of devices without worrying about compatibility issues. This universality makes it easier for users to integrate their existing peripherals into their workflows.

Thunderbolt 5: The Next Generation

With the introduction of Thunderbolt 5, Apple takes connectivity to new heights. Expected to be featured in the higher-end models of the MacBook Pro, Thunderbolt 5 offers several enhancements over its predecessor:

1. **Increased Bandwidth**: Thunderbolt 5 provides an impressive bandwidth boost, offering up to **120 Gbps** with its Bandwidth Boost feature. This increase allows for faster data transfers and improved performance when using high-bandwidth peripherals.

2. **Enhanced Display Capabilities**: With support for **DisplayPort 2.1**, Thunderbolt 5 enables connections to multiple high-resolution displays, including support for up to three **6K displays** at 60Hz or a single

display with resolutions exceeding **10K**. This capability is invaluable for professionals in fields such as video production and graphic design who require multiple screens for multitasking.

3. **Improved Power Delivery**: Thunderbolt 5 can deliver up to **240W** of power, which is particularly beneficial for charging larger devices like laptops or powering demanding peripherals such as external GPUs.

4. **Advanced Protocol Support**: The new standard supports advanced protocols like PCIe 4.0, allowing faster data access speeds for storage devices and peripherals. This enhancement ensures that users can take full advantage of high-speed storage solutions, further optimizing their workflows.

Other Ports: HDMI, SDXC, and MagSafe

In addition to the advanced Thunderbolt ports, the 2024 MacBook Pro includes several other essential connectivity options that enhance its versatility and usability:

HDMI Port

The inclusion of an HDMI port in the MacBook Pro marks a return to a beloved feature that many users have missed in previous models:

- **Display Connectivity**: The HDMI port allows users to connect their MacBook Pro directly to external monitors, TVs, or projectors without needing additional adapters or dongles. This feature simplifies presentations and media consumption by providing a straightforward way to share content on larger screens.

- **High-Resolution Support**: The HDMI port supports resolutions up to **8K**, making it suitable for high-definition content playback and professional presentations that require crisp visuals.

- **Ease of Use**: Located conveniently on the right side of the device, the HDMI port provides quick access for users who frequently switch between different display setups—whether at home or in professional environments.

SDXC Card Reader

The return of the SDXC card reader is another welcome addition that caters specifically to creative professionals:

- **Direct Media Access**: Photographers and videographers can easily insert SD cards from their cameras directly into the MacBook Pro without needing external card readers or adapters. This direct access streamlines workflows by allowing users to quickly transfer images and videos for editing.

- **Fast Data Transfer Speeds**: The SDXC card reader supports high-speed data transfer rates, ensuring that large files can be imported quickly and efficiently—essential for professionals working with high-resolution media.

- **Convenient Location**: Positioned on the right side alongside other ports, the SDXC card reader offers easy access without cluttering the workspace with additional cables or devices.

MagSafe Charging Port

Apple's decision to reintroduce the MagSafe charging port has been met with enthusiasm from long-time Mac users:

- **Magnetic Connection**: The MagSafe connector uses magnets to attach securely to the laptop, providing a reliable connection that prevents accidental disconnections—an essential feature for users who often move around while plugged in.

- **Fast Charging Capabilities**: The MagSafe port supports fast charging, allowing users to charge their MacBook Pro up to **50% in just 30 minutes**. This quick charging capability is particularly useful for professionals who need to recharge their devices rapidly between meetings or during travel.

- **Safety Features**: In addition to preventing accidental disconnections, MagSafe also protects both the charging cable and port from damage if someone trips over the cord—a thoughtful design consideration that enhances user safety.

The connectivity options available on the 2024 MacBook Pro reflect Apple's commitment to meeting the diverse needs of its user base while enhancing overall usability. With advanced Thunderbolt 4 and upcoming Thunderbolt 5 ports offering unparalleled speed and versatility, users can easily connect high-performance peripherals and multiple displays without compromising performance.

The inclusion of essential ports like HDMI and SDXC further enriches the user experience by providing straightforward solutions for connecting external displays and accessing media directly from cameras—features that are particularly valuable for creative professionals.

Moreover, the return of MagSafe charging emphasizes Apple's focus on user-friendly design and safety while delivering fast charging capabilities essential for modern workflows.

As technology continues to evolve rapidly, these connectivity options ensure that the MacBook Pro remains at the forefront of innovation—empowering users across various fields with tools designed not only for performance but also for seamless integration into their daily lives. Whether you're a creative professional needing extensive display support or an everyday user looking for reliable connectivity options, the 2024 MacBook Pro delivers an exceptional experience tailored to your needs.

Chapter 6: Battery Life and Efficiency

Battery Performance Claims

The 2024 MacBook Pro, powered by Apple's cutting-edge M4 chip, has set new standards in battery performance and efficiency, promising users an exceptional experience that combines power with longevity. Apple has long been recognized for its commitment to optimizing battery life in its devices, and the M4 chip takes this commitment to new heights.

All-Day Battery Life

Apple claims that the 2024 MacBook Pro can deliver **up to 24 hours of battery life** on a single charge. This impressive figure is made possible through a combination of advanced hardware and software optimizations. The M4 chip's architecture is designed to maximize energy efficiency while delivering high performance, allowing users to engage in demanding tasks without worrying about battery drain.

For professionals who rely on their laptops for extended periods—such as video editors, software developers, or graphic designers—the ability to work throughout the day without needing to recharge is invaluable. The M4 chip achieves this by intelligently managing power consumption based on workload demands. When performing light tasks such as web browsing or document editing, the chip operates primarily on its efficiency cores, which consume significantly less power than the performance cores.

Real-World Testing

In real-world scenarios, users have reported that the 2024 MacBook Pro consistently delivers battery life that meets or exceeds Apple's claims. For instance, during extensive video editing sessions or while running resource-intensive applications, users have noted that the laptop maintains a robust battery level, allowing for uninterrupted workflow. This reliability is particularly crucial for professionals who may not always have access to power outlets during meetings or while traveling.

Additionally, Apple has implemented features such as **Optimized Battery Charging**, which learns user charging habits and reduces battery aging by limiting the time the laptop spends fully charged. This feature ensures that the battery remains healthy over time, contributing to the overall longevity of the device.

Performance-per-Watt Efficiency of the M4 Chip

One of the most significant advancements introduced with the M4 chip is its remarkable **performance-per-watt efficiency**. This metric measures how much computational power a chip can deliver relative to its energy consumption—a critical factor for mobile devices where battery life is paramount.

Architectural Innovations

The M4 chip is built using **second-generation 3-nanometer technology**, which allows for a higher transistor density while reducing power consumption. With approximately **28 billion transistors**, this architecture enables the M4 to achieve exceptional performance levels without drawing excessive power. Apple claims that the M4 can deliver performance equivalent to that of its predecessor, the M2 while consuming only **half the power**.

When compared to contemporary PC chips found in thin and light laptops, the M4 offers similar performance using just **a quarter of the power**. This significant advantage positions Apple's silicon as a leader in energy-efficient computing—an essential consideration for users who prioritize both performance and sustainability.

Dynamic Caching and Power Management

The M4 chip incorporates several innovative features designed to enhance its efficiency further:

1. **Dynamic Caching**: This technology optimizes memory usage by allocating resources based on real-time demands. By dynamically adjusting how much memory is utilized at any given moment, the M4 can maximize performance during intensive tasks while conserving energy during lighter workloads.

2. **Intelligent Power Management**: The architecture of the M4 allows for intelligent switching between performance and efficiency cores based on workload requirements. For example, when performing simple tasks like checking email or browsing the web, the chip predominantly utilizes its efficiency cores. However, when engaging in more demanding activities such as video rendering or gaming, it seamlessly transitions to using its high-performance cores.

3. **Neural Engine Enhancements**: The M4's Neural Engine is capable of performing up to **38 trillion operations per second**, making it one of the most powerful neural processing units available today. This capability allows for complex AI tasks to be executed efficiently without straining system resources or draining battery life.

Benchmarking Performance-per-Watt

Benchmarks indicate that the M4 chip not only excels in raw performance but also maintains a competitive edge in terms of energy efficiency across various applications:

- In graphics-intensive scenarios such as gaming or video rendering, users can expect up to **four times faster GPU performance** compared to previous generations while consuming significantly less power.
- For CPU-intensive tasks like compiling code or processing large datasets, the M4 chip delivers up to **1.5 times faster CPU performance** than its predecessor while still adhering to stringent power consumption standards.

These benchmarks highlight how Apple's focus on optimizing both hardware and software contributes to an overall user experience that prioritizes efficiency without compromising on capability.

Sustainability Considerations

The advancements in battery life and efficiency also align with Apple's broader commitment to sustainability. By designing chips that consume less power while delivering high performance, Apple reduces overall energy consumption across its product lineup:

- **Reduced Carbon Footprint**: The energy-efficient design of the M4 chip contributes to lower greenhouse gas emissions associated with electricity generation over time.

- **Longer Device Lifespan**: By enhancing battery longevity through intelligent charging practices and efficient power management systems, users can enjoy their devices longer without needing replacements—further minimizing electronic waste.

- **Recyclable Materials**: Apple continues to prioritize using recycled materials in its products, ensuring that even as technology advances, environmental responsibility remains at the forefront.

The 2024 MacBook Pro represents a significant leap forward in battery life and efficiency thanks to Apple's innovative M4 chip. With claims of up to 24 hours of usage on a single charge and remarkable performance-per-watt efficiency, this device caters perfectly to professionals who demand reliability without sacrificing power.

Through architectural innovations such as dynamic caching and intelligent power management systems, combined with a commitment to sustainability, Apple has set a new standard for what users can expect from their laptops in terms of both performance and environmental responsibility.

As users embrace this latest iteration of MacBook Pro technology powered by the M4 chip, they will find themselves equipped with tools capable of handling even the most demanding tasks—while enjoying exceptional battery life that keeps them productive throughout their day-to-day activities. In an era where energy efficiency is more crucial than ever, Apple continues leading by example with solutions designed not only for today but also for a sustainable future.

Chapter 7: Camera and Multimedia Features

Upgraded Camera Specifications

The 2024 MacBook Pro introduces significant enhancements to its camera system, reflecting Apple's commitment to providing users with high-quality multimedia capabilities. The upgraded camera specifications are particularly relevant in today's digital landscape, where video conferencing, content creation, and remote collaboration have become integral to both professional and personal interactions.

High-Resolution Camera

At the forefront of these upgrades is the **12MP front-facing camera**, which offers improved image quality and clarity. This camera is designed to capture high-resolution images and videos, making it ideal for video calls, streaming, and content creation. The increased pixel count allows for better detail reproduction, ensuring that users appear sharp and clear during video conferences or when recording videos.

Enhanced Low-Light Performance

One of the standout features of the upgraded camera is its enhanced low-light performance. With advanced sensor technology and improved image processing capabilities, the camera can deliver vibrant images even in challenging lighting conditions. This enhancement is particularly beneficial for users who frequently find themselves in less-than-ideal lighting situations—such as working from home in the evening or participating in virtual meetings in dimly lit environments.

Apple has integrated sophisticated algorithms that optimize exposure and reduce noise, resulting in clearer images with better color accuracy. This improvement means that users no longer need to rely solely on external lighting setups to achieve professional-looking video quality.

Advanced Image Signal Processor (ISP)

The upgraded camera system is complemented by an advanced **Image Signal Processor (ISP)**, which plays a crucial role in enhancing image quality through real-time processing. The ISP utilizes machine learning algorithms to analyze each frame captured by the camera, making adjustments to improve focus, exposure, and color balance dynamically.

This intelligent processing allows for features such as **Smart HDR**, which combines multiple exposures to create a single image with a wider dynamic range. As a result, users can capture stunning photos with rich details in both highlights and shadows—ideal for photographers looking to achieve professional-grade results without needing additional equipment.

Center Stage and Desk View Modes

In addition to hardware improvements, the 2024 MacBook Pro introduces innovative software features that further enhance the user experience during video calls and presentations. Two of the most notable features are **Center Stage** and **Desk View**, both of which leverage the capabilities of the upgraded camera system to provide unique functionalities.

Center Stage: Keeping You In Frame

Center Stage is a groundbreaking feature designed to keep users centered in the frame during video calls. Utilizing advanced facial recognition technology and machine learning algorithms, Center Stage automatically adjusts the camera's field of view as users move around within its range. This feature is particularly useful for individuals who prefer standing desks or those who tend to move around while speaking.

- **Dynamic Framing**: As users shift positions or turn their heads during a call, Center Stage intelligently pans and zooms to ensure they remain at the center of the frame. This dynamic framing creates a more engaging experience for participants on the other end of the call, fostering better communication and connection.

- **Group Calls**: In addition to individual use, Center Stage can accommodate multiple participants by adjusting its framing based on the number of people present in front of the camera. This capability makes it ideal for group meetings or collaborative sessions where several individuals may be interacting simultaneously.

- **User-Friendly Experience**: The feature is easy to enable through system settings or video conferencing applications. Users can simply toggle it on or off as needed, allowing for flexibility depending on their preferences during different types of calls.

Desk View: Showcasing Your Workspace

Another innovative addition is **Desk View**, which leverages the ultra-wide capabilities of the MacBook Pro's camera system. This feature allows users to showcase their desk space during video calls, making it an invaluable tool for educators, presenters, or anyone looking to share physical materials with their audience.

- **Dual Perspective**: Desk View enables users to display both their face and their workspace simultaneously. By utilizing an ultra-wide lens configuration, this mode captures a broader view that includes not only the user but also any documents, sketches, or objects placed on their desk.

- **Enhanced Collaboration**: For professionals who frequently conduct presentations or workshops remotely, Desk View offers an effective way to engage with participants by allowing them to see both visual aids and the presenter's expressions. This dual perspective enhances communication and understanding during discussions.

- **Setup Requirements**: To use Desk View effectively, users may need additional setup steps within their video conferencing software. However, once configured, it provides a seamless way to integrate physical materials into virtual interactions without requiring complicated arrangements or additional cameras.

Multimedia Capabilities

The upgraded camera specifications combined with innovative features like Center Stage and Desk View position the 2024 MacBook Pro as a powerful tool for multimedia applications beyond just video conferencing:

1. **Content Creation**: Creators can leverage the high-resolution camera for streaming platforms or social media content creation. The ability to capture high-quality video with enhanced low-light performance ensures that creators can produce professional-grade content from virtually anywhere.

2. **Educational Use**: Educators can utilize Desk View during remote teaching sessions to share whiteboards or physical materials with students effectively. This capability fosters interactive learning experiences that engage students more deeply than traditional methods.

3. **Virtual Events**: For professionals involved in hosting webinars or virtual events, having access to high-quality video capabilities enhances audience engagement. The combination of Center Stage and Desk View allows hosts to maintain a professional appearance while effectively showcasing relevant materials.

4. **Social Connectivity**: In an era where social interaction often occurs online, having access to advanced camera features enhances personal connections through platforms like FaceTime or Zoom. Users can enjoy richer interactions with friends and family through improved video quality and dynamic framing options.

The 2024 MacBook Pro's upgraded camera specifications and innovative multimedia features represent a significant advancement in how users engage with technology for communication and content creation. With a high-resolution camera capable of delivering exceptional image quality even in low-light conditions, combined with intelligent features like Center Stage and Desk View, Apple has positioned this device as an essential tool for professionals and creatives alike.

As remote work continues to be a prevalent aspect of modern life, having access to advanced multimedia capabilities enhances not only productivity but also personal connections. Whether you're conducting business meetings, teaching classes online, or creating engaging content for social media platforms, the 2024 MacBook Pro equips you with tools designed to elevate your experience—ensuring that you always look your best while staying connected with others.

In summary, Apple's commitment to enhancing user experience through cutting-edge technology shines through in every aspect of the 2024 MacBook Pro's camera system. These advancements empower users across various fields by providing them with high-quality tools that facilitate effective communication and creative expression in today's digital landscape.

Chapter 8: Pricing and Availability

Price Points for Each Model

The 2024 MacBook Pro lineup, featuring Apple's latest M4 chip, has generated considerable excitement among tech enthusiasts and professionals alike. With three distinct models available, each tailored to meet varying performance needs and budgets, Apple continues to uphold its reputation for quality and innovation in the laptop market. Here's a detailed breakdown of the price points for each model:

1. **14-Inch MacBook Pro with M4**:
   - **Starting Price**: $1,599
   - This entry-level model is designed for everyday users who require a reliable device for tasks such as web browsing, document editing, and light media consumption. Equipped with a 10-core CPU and a 10-core GPU, it provides ample power for general use while maintaining energy efficiency.

2. **14-Inch MacBook Pro with M4 Pro**:
   - **Starting Price**: $1,999
   - Aimed at professionals who engage in more demanding workloads, this model features a 14-core CPU and up to a 20-core GPU. It is well-suited for tasks like video editing, graphic design, and software development. The increased memory options (up to 64GB) make it an excellent choice for multitasking and running resource-intensive applications.

3. **16-Inch MacBook Pro with M4 Pro**:
   - **Starting Price**: $2,499
   - This larger variant offers similar specifications to the 14-inch model but provides additional screen real estate for users who prefer working with multiple windows or require higher resolution for detailed graphics work.

4. **14-Inch MacBook Pro with M4 Max**:
   - **Starting Price**: $2,499
   - This model is designed for power users who demand the highest performance levels. Featuring a 16-core CPU and a 40-core GPU, it excels in graphics-intensive applications such as 3D rendering and complex data analysis. Users can configure this model with up to 128GB of unified memory.

5. **16-Inch MacBook Pro with M4 Max**:
   - **Starting Price**: $2,999
   - The flagship model combines the most powerful specifications available in the MacBook Pro lineup. With its robust hardware configuration, it is tailored for professionals in fields like animation, video production, and scientific research.

Preorder Details and Release Dates

Apple has made the preorder process straightforward and accessible for customers eager to get their hands on the new MacBook Pro models. Here are the key details regarding preorder availability and release dates:

Preorder Availability

- **Preorders Opened**: Preorders for the 2024 MacBook Pro models began on October 30, 2024.
- Customers can place their orders directly through Apple's website or authorized retailers. The preorder process allows users to secure their preferred model before the official release date.

Expected Release Dates

- **Official Launch Date**: The new MacBook Pro models are set to be officially released on November 8, 2024.
- Following the launch date, customers who pre-ordered will receive their devices promptly, while general availability will extend to retail locations and online platforms.

Market Positioning and Comparisons

The pricing of the 2024 MacBook Pro models positions them competitively within the premium laptop market. When compared to similar offerings from competitors such as Dell's XPS series or Microsoft's Surface Laptop lineup, Apple's pricing reflects its commitment to high-quality materials, innovative technology, and a seamless user experience.

Value Proposition

1. **Performance vs. Cost**: While the initial price points may appear steep compared to entry-level laptops from other brands, the performance capabilities of the M4 chip—especially in multitasking scenarios—justify the investment for

professionals who rely on their devices for demanding tasks.

2. **Longevity and Resale Value**: Apple products are known for their longevity and strong resale value. Investing in a MacBook Pro typically means that users can expect several years of reliable performance without significant degradation in functionality.

3. **Ecosystem Integration**: For users already invested in the Apple ecosystem—such as iPhones or iPads—the seamless integration across devices enhances overall productivity and user experience. Features like Handoff, AirDrop, and Universal Clipboard further solidify Apple's value proposition.

The pricing structure of the 2024 MacBook Pro lineup reflects Apple's commitment to delivering high-performance devices tailored to meet diverse user needs—from casual users seeking reliability to professionals requiring top-tier performance capabilities. With starting prices ranging from $1,599 to $2,999 depending on the model and configuration chosen, Apple continues to position itself as a leader in the premium laptop market.

The preorder process has been streamlined for customer convenience, allowing eager buyers to secure their devices ahead of the official launch on November 8, 2024. As anticipation builds around these new models equipped with the innovative M4 chip, users can look forward to enhanced performance capabilities that cater specifically to their professional demands.

In summary, whether you are a creative professional looking for powerful graphics capabilities or an everyday user needing a reliable laptop for daily tasks, the 2024 MacBook Pro lineup offers compelling options that deliver exceptional value through advanced technology and seamless integration within Apple's ecosystem. As always, investing in an Apple product means not just acquiring a device but also gaining access to an unparalleled user experience that prioritizes quality, performance, and innovation at every turn.

Conclusion

Summary of Key Features

The 2024 MacBook Pro lineup, powered by Apple's groundbreaking M4 chip, represents a significant leap forward in portable computing technology. With three distinct models—the 14-inch MacBook Pro with M4, the 14-inch and 16-inch MacBook Pro with M4 Pro, and the 14-inch and 16-inch MacBook Pro with M4 Max—Apple has tailored its offerings to meet the diverse needs of users ranging from everyday consumers to high-performance professionals.

1. **M4 Chip Architecture**

At the heart of the new MacBook Pro is the M4 chip, built on a second-generation 3-nanometer process that integrates a powerful 10-core CPU and a robust GPU configuration. The M4 chip delivers exceptional performance-per-watt efficiency, allowing users to engage in demanding tasks without sacrificing battery life. This architecture not only enhances speed and responsiveness but also maintains energy efficiency, providing users with up to **24 hours of battery life** on a single charge.

2. **Enhanced Graphics Performance**

The GPU capabilities of the M4 chip are particularly noteworthy. The entry-level M4 model features a **10-core GPU**, while the M4 Pro and M4 Max models offer up to **20-core** and **40-core GPUs**, respectively. This significant increase in graphical power enables professionals working in fields such as video editing, 3D rendering, and game development to achieve stunning visual fidelity and smooth performance across demanding applications.

3. **Advanced Camera System**

The upgraded camera system includes a **12MP front-facing camera** that excels in low-light conditions, enhanced by an advanced Image Signal Processor (ISP). Features like **Center Stage** and **Desk View** transform video conferencing experiences by keeping users centered in the frame and allowing them to showcase their workspace effectively. These enhancements cater to the growing demand for high-quality video communication in both professional and personal contexts.

4. **Connectivity Options**

The inclusion of Thunderbolt 4 and Thunderbolt 5 ports enhances connectivity options significantly. Users can connect multiple high-resolution displays, and daisy-chain devices, and enjoy fast data transfer rates of up to **120 Gbps** with Thunderbolt 5. Additionally, traditional ports like HDMI and SDXC card readers have been reintroduced, catering to creative professionals who require versatile connectivity solutions.

5. **Innovative Multimedia Features**

The MacBook Pro lineup incorporates innovative multimedia capabilities that enhance user experience. The combination of an upgraded camera system with advanced software features allows for seamless transitions between personal and professional use cases. Whether it's streaming content or conducting virtual meetings, users can expect high-quality performance across various scenarios.

6. **Pricing Structure**

With starting prices ranging from **$1,599** for the base model to **$2,999** for the flagship M4 Max model, Apple has positioned its MacBook Pro lineup competitively within the premium laptop market. The pricing reflects not only the advanced technology but also the longevity and resale value associated with Apple products.

Future Implications for Users and Developers

As we look ahead, the advancements introduced with the 2024 MacBook Pro have significant implications for both users and developers across various fields:

Empowering Professionals

1. **Enhanced Productivity**: The combination of powerful hardware and intelligent software optimizations empowers professionals to work more efficiently than ever before. With improved performance-per-watt efficiency, users can engage in multitasking without experiencing slowdowns or

interruptions—whether they are editing videos, compiling code, or conducting research.

2. **Creative Innovation**: For creative professionals—such as graphic designers, video editors, and animators—the enhanced graphics capabilities open up new possibilities for innovation. The ability to render high-quality visuals in real time allows creators to push boundaries in their work, resulting in richer content that captivates audiences.

3. **Remote Collaboration**: As remote work continues to be a prevalent aspect of modern life, features like Center Stage and Desk View facilitate effective communication during virtual meetings. Professionals can present their ideas more dynamically while maintaining engagement with colleagues or clients—enhancing collaboration regardless of physical location.

Developer Opportunities

1. **Expanding Software Ecosystem**: With the introduction of Apple Intelligence—powered by the advanced Neural Engine—developers have new opportunities to create applications that leverage AI capabilities

directly on devices. This shift enables more sophisticated applications that can perform complex tasks locally without relying on cloud processing.

2. **Focus on Performance Optimization**: Developers will need to adapt their applications to take full advantage of the M4 chip's architecture and performance characteristics. Optimizing software for Apple's silicon means creating applications that can seamlessly utilize both performance and efficiency cores based on user needs.

3. **Cross-Platform Development**: As Apple continues to integrate its ecosystem across devices—from iPhones to iPads—the opportunities for cross-platform development expand significantly. Developers can create applications that work seamlessly across multiple devices while leveraging shared capabilities such as Handoff or Universal Clipboard.

Sustainability Considerations

Apple's commitment to sustainability is evident in its design philosophy for the 2024 MacBook Pro lineup. By focusing on energy-efficient technology and using recycled materials in production, Apple sets an example for other tech companies regarding environmental responsibility:

1. **Longer Device Lifespan**: The emphasis on battery longevity through intelligent charging practices ensures that devices remain functional longer, reducing electronic waste—a critical consideration as consumers become increasingly conscious of their environmental impact.

2. **Reduced Carbon Footprint**: By optimizing power consumption through advanced chip architecture, Apple contributes to lower greenhouse gas emissions associated with electricity generation over time—aligning with global sustainability goals.

The 2024 MacBook Pro lineup is not just an incremental upgrade; it represents a transformative leap in technology that redefines what users can expect from portable computing devices. With its powerful M4 chip at the core, enhanced graphics capabilities, upgraded camera features, versatile connectivity options, and innovative multimedia functionalities, Apple has created a device that meets the demands of today's professionals while preparing them for future challenges.

For users seeking exceptional performance combined with reliability, the new MacBook Pro models deliver an unparalleled experience tailored specifically to their needs—whether they are casual users looking for efficiency or power users requiring cutting-edge technology for demanding tasks.

As we move forward into an increasingly digital world where remote collaboration and creative innovation are paramount, the implications of these advancements extend far beyond individual use cases; they shape how we interact with technology as a whole.

In summary, Apple's commitment to excellence shines through every aspect of the 2024 MacBook Pro lineup—empowering users across various fields while paving the way for future developments in computing technology that prioritize performance, sustainability, and user experience at every turn. As this new era unfolds, one thing is clear: the future is bright for those who embrace these powerful tools designed not just for today but also for tomorrow's challenges and opportunities.

www.ingramcontent.com/pod-product-compliance
Lightning Source LLC
Chambersburg PA
CBHW071305050326
40690CB00011B/2530